I AM HOMELAND

TWELVE KOREAN-AMERICAN POETS

EDITED BY YEARN HONG CHOI

POETIC MATRIX PRESS

Cover painting by Euna Park

ISBN: 978-0-9860600-0-7

Poetic Matrix Press
www.poeticmatrix.com

ACKNOWLEGEMENTS

The Poetic Matrix Press Publisher and the editor of this poetry book thank J. Glenn Evans for his words on the back cover of this book.

Dr. Seo acknowledges his first eight poems were originally translated by Professor Nanhae Kim from Korean into English and published in his Korean poetry book, *Gracious Maria*. They were revised by Seo himself for this anthology.

Dr. Choi thanks *Poetry Pacific* for permission to reuse "Ode to Sleep" and the *Pen* (Poetry Explosion Network) to reuse "Kitchen" for this anthology. Mr. Sibok Kim translated "Ode to Sleep" from Korean into English.

Mr. Hogill Kim's 10 poems in this volume are selected from his forthcoming poetry book, *Desert Poems*.

PREFACE

ST. JAMES WAY

The first martyred body sailed to Spain from Jerusalem via the Mediterranean Sea where he spent his life spreading the Word of Jesus. Angels must have guided his boat as there was no sailor or mast to guide the boat.

A horse on the beach was the first to discover the arrival of the martyred body and, in surprise, jumped into the waters. Miraculously, the martyred rose and rescued the horse from the water, only to fall back into the sea. His body was covered by scallop shells. Then, the horse rescued the martyred body, carrying him to an inland spot. His followers buried his body. A star emerged over his gravesite, the Santiago de Compostela.

His followers made the 900 kilometer pilgrimage in his footsteps, following the trails of shells. They began in Saint Jean Pied de Port in France, climbed the Pyrenees, walked along the country and town roads to Santiago de Compostela and to Finisterre, where the martyred body arrived by a boat.

They all witnessed the waves at the end of St. James' road. Buen Camino!

Sorrow
—at the deaths of the young and their teachers at Sandy Hook Elementary School

Weapons are the tools of violence;
All decent men detest them. Tao Te Ching #31

Sorrow makes humankind one and cleans each other's tears.

Sorrow touches the most painful wounds like a mother's hands.

Sorrow is not the most beautiful thing, but that which soothes and heals the wounds.

The 20 young children who did not yet know what death was, and six teachers who tried to protect their lives, were killed by a mental patient.

Their deaths dictate to us to remove the guns from our world.

They still speak to us:

Please remove the guns from our world.

Yearn Hong Choi, editor

Contents

INTRODUCTION

Korean poets in this poetry book are the first generation immigrants to the United States. They speak and write the Korean language among themselves. The mother tongue comforts even those who have been living more or less than half a century in the United States. English can never be their mother tongue. English is still their second language. They speak English in the American society. Most often their English, or vocabulary power, is limited when writing their poems in English, so they write their poems in Korean and translate them into English. Of course, some command English very well. They are not in this volume. This book is a poetry book in translation. Limited English hampers the quality of poetry in English, but they love poetry and are proud of their creative writing endeavors. Poets in this anthology have not yet published in the *New Yorker* and *The Atlantic*, but their dreams and hopes are there. First of all, they should not be discriminated against.

The Second and the third generation of Korean-American poets may not identify themselves as Korean poets. They are already part of the American mainstream. However, first-generation Korean poets must be recognized as the border-land people between Korea and the United States. They are neither Korean nor American. In a real sense, they are Korean-American. As the editor of this book, and as a Korean-American poet myself, I believe that writing in one's native language in America is not enough; translating the poems into English is a must. Some loss in translation is understandable, but even translated poems can show the breadth and depth of Korean-American people's nostalgia, grief and pain, homesickness, and joy of life in lyricism. Their life in the American political, social, economic and cultural space is of course reflected in their poetry. They are living in their American setting with nostalgia and homesickness. They are cross-cultural beings. Their poetry also demonstrates their love of their family—parents and children. Their poetry are love letters to their love for persons and objects.

In the 1960s, I was a young foreign student at Indiana University. My town friends (as opposed to the Greek House people), the liberal political force on campus, published my poems in English in their underground weekly newspaper. They encouraged me, "Your poems are great. Your poems are beautiful." They welcomed my poems because foreign students had every right to express their literary thoughts in its newspaper. They denied that poetry was just for English majors.

I continued my poetry with limited English. English has never become my language. In the 1980s, I met Gwendolyn Brooks, the first Black Pulitzer poet, who also encouraged me to continue my poetry writing. She told me: "You are a good poet. Don't be discouraged even if your poems are not published by a major publishing house."

She has sustained my life in the United States as a poet. She is the motivating force behind this anthology. I have edited two Korean-American poetry books, and want to continue to do so, because Korean immigrants love writing poetry in which they can express the beauty of the "dailyness of life"—small, sparkling moments that pass everyday, some paeans, some promises, and some pleas.

I present this book as the voice of Korean-American poets to the United States and to the world. Poetry inspires me and my fellow Korean poets in America every day because it is beautiful and more glorious than the prose world I know. We want to show our presence, first of all, to our neighbors.

One final note: I don't claim that this book represents all Korean-American poets. There are more than one hundred Korean poets across the United States. Poets in this volume are my close friends and/or associates.

Yearn Hong Choi, Ph.D.
Founding President
The Korean-American Poets Group

I AM HOMELAND

3/22/2016

To Mayor
RUSSULL J. LITCHULT

K—

POEMS BY BYOUNG KIE LEE

Byoung Kie Lee is a poet and medical doctor, practicing medicine for families in Maryland. He is a leading member of the Korean Poets and Writers Group in the Washington Area.

At the Serengeti National Park, Tanzania

Vast blue sky is hanging
Over the Serengeti Safari,
In which the scene of snow-covered Mt. Kilimanjaro is finally fading.

Herds of water buffalo, wild ox, zebra, elephant, giraffe, wildebeest
Are slowly approaching us, as the currents of powerful waves;
They were small dots in the distant horizon ten or fifteen minutes
    before.

They are passing by us
Who are confined to the limit of a safari jeep
Carelessly, carelessly, carelessly.

Somewhere lions, cheetahs, leopards, hyenas are hiding and looking
    for the animals
Who are dropouts of their herd;
There are always predators in the world.

Black vultures are flying over the vast blue sky, as well,
Darting, preying, snatching like a flash
The animals who are out of their herd.

Don't get out of your herd!
Don't be a dropout of your race!
Don't be far away from your group!

The meadow of the Serengeti National Park is yelling at me:
Survival of the fittest is the basic teaching of the African safari.
Don't lose your vitality. Then, you are aimed at by predators.

Ernest Hemingway may be saying the same thing to me:
Honor your parents and love thy neighbors.

MONGOL MAGPIE

Mongol magpie is crying,
Caw, caw, caw...

Untying her long dark hair and replacing new clean water from the
    spring every morning,
She was praying for her parents, family and country in Mongolia.

Mother, take care of yourself.
I am fine. My Mongol husband is taking care of me well.
So you don't need to cry for me.
Don't worry about me.

She was crying as magpie was crying
As if vomiting blood
During her life time
In a tent village on the meadow
Toward the naked mountain in the South.

Naked mountain over another naked mountain,
Surrounding her,
Made a prisoner of the Korea Kingdom
Conquered by Ginghis Khan
In the 15th century.

She became a magpie in Mongolia.

MOUNTAIN ECHO

Sleepy deer drinking water in the creek.
Is he enjoying the morning ritual?
He is now licking the waist line of the mountain.

While he is eating the bamboo shoots, and
Watching the hill before him,
The sun rises again over the top of the mountain.

In the night,
He pours the starlight into the crystal bowl,
Drops flower petals under the bowl.
His peaceful prayer is dissolved into the bowl.

HOLY SPIRIT

No one doubts the presence of Oxygen,
But some doubt Your presence.

Inside the woods, near the creek where birds sing as an orchestra,
I breathe abundance of Oxygen.
There I feel your presence.

I remember the first date with a young beautiful woman
In my twenties.
So exciting, so long ago.
Then, I forgot her precious presence to my life.

I have grown up in the sacred world
After a long sailing of stormy seas.

I re-discover her presence and
Your presence.

Thank you, my Lord.

MOTHER

She was just an 18-year-old lady
Raised by her loving parents
As the precious gift to them
When she married a young man in the country.

She married into a large clan of the landlord gentry class.
She made fire every morning for their breakfast,
After drawing up drinking and cooking water from the community well.

She washed the clothes of all family members
In the cold icy water in the winter season.
She resisted sleepy nights to sew dresses for the family members
Under the candle light.

She protected her young son with her feeble body
From the enemy bombing of the country house.

She moved to the city
When her son moved to receive middle school education.
She earned money for his education at college level.

She moved to the United States
When her son immigrated to the land of new opportunity.
Then, she learned A, B, C, D......X, Y, Z
As a senior citizen.
She became an elementary school girl.

Then, she received her driver's license and gave rides to all her
    grandchildren.
She was loved by her grandchildren, friends and neighbors.

She passed away.

Her 45-year life as Josephine in the Catholic Church
With the Lord was a blessing
Was witnessed by the Region Marie Catena,

But I cried, because I could not fill the void she left in this world.

SETTLEMENT

I came to the United States of America
with a few coins in my pocket.
I purchased a house, and planted trees and spread out mulch
under the trees. After years of labor, I became a middle class American.

I am the first Lee grandpa of the Silver Spring, Maryland Lee clan.

There is a General Lee's clan in Virginia.
Ha, Ha, ha

BORN, 1945

I was born in a Korean farm house in the last year of the Pacific War
or in the year of Liberation from the Japanese yoke.

I grew up in the barley hill, survived the Korean War,
and witnessed the Korean modernization campaign.

Now, I realize I am the last analogue generation fellow
in front of innocent grandsons in the United States of America.

I COULD NOT SAY GOODBYE

My good neighbor from Korea,
Mrs. Lim, was killed by a gunman in her store
Who was seeking a few dollars from her hands.

Robbery for a few dollars killed one immigrant's dream.
Is it real, possible?
She was a kind, nice and generous woman
With a smile on her face.

How could a young man aim at her life?

I could not say, Goodbye, to her at her funeral.
Tears could not make my eyes unable to see her.

God bless Mrs. Lim!
She had a dream to buy her own house
After selling the store
In the District of Columbia.

AT LAKE TITICACA

My ancestors crossed the Bering Sea once,
Walked the North American continent,
And settled down at the Andes Mountains.
Some built reed houses inside Lake Titicaca
In order to avoid the Spaniard rule.
Each house was made of the reed,
And each island was made of the reed.
Uros, a group of 44 or so artificial islands made of floating reeds, totora.
The Uros chief invited us to his house decorated by famous Korean
Actors and actresses.
Wow, they greeted us.
The round face, black hair, brown-tanned island people on the lake
Were all my relatives, sharing the same ancestors.
Their smiling faces could be seen in my home country.
Their happiness with food from roots of reed and fish from the lake
Shone over their primitive life.
They showed us: happiness has nothing to do with modern civilization.
Their Arirang waves lasted until our reed boat landed at the shore.

ON KOREAN POLITICS

All the exam questions were answered in a multiple choice or OX
    format.
All Korean people were well trained for that kind of exam.

Two young middle school girls were killed by the U.S. amphibious
    vehicle.
The Korean response to the tragic accident was: "Yankee, go home!"
Then, who can defend South Korea from the North Korean threat?
Candle light demonstrations were going on and on for months.

The U.S. exported mad-cow meats to Korea.
The Korean response to such ridiculous biased television news was:
"No more import from the U.S.!"
Then, who can sell Korean products to the U.S. market?
Candle light demonstrations were going on and on for months.

Thousands of U.S. soldiers were killed in unknown war fields.
Did the Korean people forget the Korean War and accuse the killers
    of two young girls?
The export-oriented Korean economy made Korea the #11 world
    economic powerhouse.
Did the Korean people forget the Korean economy's life-line and
    remember the mad-cow disease?

The leftist Korean political leaders should be able to answer in O or X.
Pathetic O or pathetic X.

Poems by Chun U Yi

Chun U Yi is a poet and essayist. He has two poetry books in Korean, *Time Need Rest* and *Between Spring and Summer.*

LIKE A DOG, LIKE AN OX

When called upon with a Hey!
I ran over like a dog and
worked like an ox.
Like an ox, I smiled an idiot smile,
uttering okay, okay all day.
I worked as ordered and received when given.
As a naked being, I became an ox to survive.
I couldn't take off the rein.
I had to work without weekends
Since the rein was my lifeline.

There was no hill to graze, or inherited land or a house.
I gathered my wife, children, and a bundle of luggage and came over.
It is said that a day in a day is satisfactory.
But the ox has to hurriedly and hastily run.
Hence I became a dog who sniffs out the odor of money.
From a factory, where fingers go missing,
from the stench of the garbage, out came the odor of money.

As it is my duty to be a provider,
Whilst I listened to the sound of my breaking,
I have become an ox.
When the colts frolic on the green hills,
the ox will calculate the profit and loss.

FORSYTHIA

When a child, grown commandingly over the winter,
goes to the playground, holding on to grandma's hand,
Forsythia Flowers Bloom and the Leaves Wither as the heat simmers
in haze, a forsythia blossom bloomed.

As the grandma, dazed by its golden splendor, walks away,
the child lets go of her hand and skips ahead
while the flower buds on the branches
stealthily bloom brightly one by one.

As the sun sets on the playground, a lingering winter breeze
chases the child held onto by the grandma's hand
and, while the wet hands are drying,
a forsythia blossom drops and a leaf grows.

The insensitive grandma walks with her head down
while the child, slow in keeping up,
cries loudly, the branches become dense with leaves.

As the puppy on a leash
leaps with its two paws in the air
the child wails and hides behind the grandma's legs.

The child and the puppy goes around
the street corner, the leaves forlornly wither away.

I AM HOMELAND

People ask, for my homeland.
Since I am the homeland now there can be no other.
I crossed the ocean, crossed the time, and took root, and
had children and the children had their own children.
Therefore, I am the solid homeland for the later generations.
It is the homeland waiting with bright smiles.

The stories held by the embarrassingly enlarged gourds,
on thatched roofs are gone without a trace.
The moldy family census register, deemed worthier than life itself.
The grandfathers buried forever back home,
blown here and thither by the Northern and Western winds, and the
family census register, as important as the spirit tablet, was lost.

The head of the family, who was like a pillar, was lost too.
My homeland, where grandfather's breath is long gone,
with morphed mountains and streams, lost without trace.
Since I carry the olden times,
I am the homeland.

The Woman Who Sells Bread

The day, like others, held wet fallen leaves.
In a marketplace, where many lives gather,
the woman sold bread from the left
and I sold candy from the right,
hungry people waiting for other hungry people.
In a drizzling afternoon, I make a meal
out of sweet bread.
We were united by smiles, exchanged
with hard bark like bread and
expired candy.
Although I was painfully stuffy, forever immersed in hunger,
within the intimate glances
affection and love traveled across the way.
And the fallen leaves were swept away,
I am stepping on the fallen leaves, similar and yet different,
from across the river.

I wonder if the woman, whose wish was to go to a church holding hands,
ever got her legal residency.
There is no reply when life is called upon.

A POET'S AUTUMN

Our relationship ended abruptly
like an ending of a television drama at a crucial point
with the last scene in a close-up.

While the seasons pass boisterously with heartlessness,
is reading a poem extravagance or idleness?
Similar to being curious about the end of a drama,
looking for that person in a stanza of a poem,
could be the lack of ruthlessness or tenderness of the heart.
Although the love has ended, in a destitute lingering attachment,
I want to write a touching stanza of a poem.

Could the season be blamed for the delicately rising images?
The dreams from younger days float faintly;
in the cold of the night, fallen leaves skipped through the wind,
we have felt the warmth of each other with roasted chestnuts,
and walked over the fallen leaves.

In This Autumn

Sue, "please don't be sick."
After my tumultuous heart became hollow,
I too have become a patient.
Before long, before the leaves whisper their suffering,
when the frost knocks on your heart,
the marked love will sprout.

The suffocating essence,
for the price of a bundle, as large as a house, of spring onions,
the back stiffening moan
echoed in the valley, throughout the long summer.

If there is no way to soothe the wounded heart
take a foliage sightseeing train and go into the autumn.
There are many weeping sorrows in there.
Weep along with the woman with long neck.
Lives will be comforted a bit.

Now and then,
go to a symphony and submerge into its melody
and caress the wounded time.

When the autumn wind passes through the hollow heart,
a new person would welcome you.

THE FRAGRANCE OF NEIGHBORS

The neighbors go back a long time.
Marinated with tender affection like an ancient moss,
the few friends, entangled like roots,
show their hearts without seeking faults.

There's a guy who shares all matters small and great.
There's a gal who is as sweet as a peach.
The world becomes brighter
with her constant bright smile.

Drunken with well-aged liquor,
when we talk the worldly talk,
the world becomes truly fragrant.

My dear neighbors,
the dense fragrance
is lovelier than any flower.

The Potomac River

You couldn't come to me even if you are filled with yearning,
since the time has stretched long and far away.
In the place, where I have engraved you in my eyes and my heart,
longing from a short distance,
I am no longer there.

You may weep with your longing heart from moment to moment
and I too shall feel the carved longing from my heart now and then.
But I cannot go to you.
I am afraid that it might be an awkward meeting.
I wouldn't have much to say even if I made a space for myself,
within the quickening steps of life.
No need to cleanse one's heart, with closed eyes, awaiting me.
You and I had to halt before infinite number of traffic lights
and there are more traffic lights waiting before us.

The river of love, laced with the Indian woman,
Pocahontas' spirit, the Potomac River flows from and to.
Across the river, you are in Maryland and I am in Virginia.
Even if the river is drenched with our longings,
it's the river we cannot cross,
as you stand north of the river and I stand south of the river.

THE EVENNESS

The shadow of the sun is elongated
and when the sweetness saturates the pears,
I often look out into the back yard.
The small green pepper like fruits on the date tree
tell the shy tale of still distant harvest time.
And only the smell of young green can be whiffed under the pear tree.
When looked up on my way back,
a crow is at the top of the tree, pecking on a decent looking fruit.
Knowing I can't fence the top of the tree, a family of pear thieves
is weighing down the branches of the pear tree one by one.
While the sweet pears are taken over by the crows, bees, and ants,
I am left with the bitter green pears.
Ultimately in the end, they share the pears and dates in good humor.
And when they fly away to somewhere else, pretty foliage covers
    the land.
We leave for the Shenandoah Sky Way mountains and streams.
Knowing that there's no fence there,
we roam around, stealing the images,
the images of the pretty trees, acquired by scorching all summer.

ON VACATION

Left for the three-year planned vacation.
Rain drizzled thick as noodles.
And the wind, like an edge of a sword, cuts through the rain.
The years of undulating waves,
and for how many more years,
would the waves break emitting fishy odor
pushing and pushing away the polluted foam
taking away the sand washed by the foam.
The ocean washed, white sand beach is clean
but the man washed by passing time
only feels sadness like saltwater covered flint.
The era of back bending hardship makes
the old pine tree shed his tears.

Of course, after fifty years have passed,
riding a bicycle cannot be easy.
I learn back from a five-year-old granddaughter.
Don't go too fast, go straight,
don't go to the sandy beach,
a car is following right behind you.
Like having lived with twist and turns,
I ride the bike, speeding through the rainy beach.

POEMS BY DOO HYUN CHUNG

Dr. Doo Hyun Chung is a medical doctor (radiologist) in
Maryland. Poet, painter and sculptor. His poetry book is
Reincarnation of Budapest (in Korean). He received the
Overseas Poet Award from the Yoon Dong-ju Memorial
Group in Seoul.

SEA LINE

The sacred writing authored by the sky and the sea
Only one line
Scripture
In the world

JANG MI RAN*

She lifted 319 kg over all in total,
138 kg in snatch, 181 kg in the clean and jerk
Over her head.
She lifted the world.
Heracles!
She was once a shy, slim, little country girl.

*Jang won her third straight world championship title in the
women's over 75 kg category.

O

One island
In the vast blue sea

The sky
Above

The sea
Below

There is no boundary line
Between the two

Only roundness
Only emptiness

O is round
O is empty

Inside O
Universe is hiding
Galaxy is hiding

AERIAL SEPULTURE

Wind removed flesh
Left only
White skeleton
After many more years
Than
His life endured

I was scared of
His icy cold presence
Or silence
In a hot summer day
at the top of Mt. Jiri
in the 1950s

AN EMPTY TOMB

In the midst of fire shell of the Korean War,
Vanished

My father, missing
No traces to his death

My mother,
Her husband,
Built a tomb for her husband's missing
Or death
Without his remains or ash

That was her last dedication to her beloved husband

Buried in the empty grave of my father,
The last scene of his back walking out

Inside the empty grave,
Echoes of his last footsteps in October 1950

She passed away, and so
Passed an ideological war of one generation

Do not say, it
is empty   Never

Never, never, never

PYONGYANG, 1986

At mid-night
I opened the window of my room
in the Korea Hotel
"Father ———"
I called out as loud as I could
at the top of my lungs.
The night air, shattered by
my hoarse voice.
One star fell
over the horizon.
I will dig tomorrow morning
where the meteorite landed.
My father's bones
could be there.

DANDELION AT MACHU PICCHU

The glory of the Machu Picchu is still at large;
Ruins of the stones on the hill surrounded by a river
Do not say very much to me.
The mystic ancient city could be the last Inca Emperor's summer palace
Or his last secret castle that the Spaniards could not find.
There is no written record on the ruins.
A Yale historian carried out all the treasures to the States,
And now Yale should return everything he moved out of the hill.
Today, I only see a dandelion living and surviving in the cracked stone
Next to the royal family member's house.
The same dandelion the Emperor saw must be blossomed
For a modern poet's imagination.

AT THE VIETNAM WAR MEMORIAL

One old retired soldier
in his wheel chair
in front of the black granite wall.

Tears
flowing from his two eyes
to his cheeks.

Tears
Flowing
via the human conscience
from Maine to California,
from Alaska to Florida.

See 58,261 names
on the V-shaped granite wall,
either killed or missing in action.

He touches his fingers
on his friend's engraved name.

Each name writing the modern day scripture,
Each name making the confession of
American tragedy.

Behind those tragedies,
Hear Vietnamese people's songs of victory,
See the nameless Vietnamese people and Vietcong,
Dead in their rice paddies and in their jungles.

The Andes Woman

Peruvian girls,
Growing happily with birds' chirping and the sound of water in the creek,
Playing with a new borne calf and a puppy,
Dancing with wild flowers in the high land, and
Seeding corn, potatos and wheat in the family farm in early Spring,
Harvesting them in the late autumn.
They become women and marry men grown in the same Andes valley:
Their dreams and hopes are high as the Andes Mountain.
Their children will grow up as they have been.
They do not want Western civilization on their mountain and valley.

MY MOTHER BECOMES A CAMEL

My mother becomes a camel with two humps,
crossing the desert.

After leaving the empty grave of her missing husband
and one small grave for her young son,
she is crossing the Gobi Desert.

She has dropped her living two sons and two daughters
one by one in each oasis she has reached,
and still climbs up a long sandy hill.

She is still on her barefeet and walks on the desert sand
after teaching her children where the North Star
and other constellations were,
and pushing her husband and young son to Heaven.

She is still crossing the desert sea without an oar.

Oh, my mother.

POEMS BY HYOUNG O KIM

Hyoung O Kim is a poet and small business owner in New Jersey. He has one poetry book, *Celestial Island* (in Korean).

CELESTIAL ISLAND

soaring alone
quivering again

back and forth each day
the island of many a daily capsizing

seagulls flying in flocks but
sit singly and cry alone

though in their waddles
not very different

they follow the currents floating afar
sails pitched in the sky

pushing onward
up and down as going toward

*_translated by_ Wolhee Choe, Hawks Media, New York

FROM KITCHEN

between kitchen and counter in
my deli store, wife and I
trying to cross over the cliff but
falling a hundred times a day
absorbing kids' complaints
still looking at the
sizzling and twisting on the grill
my 25 cent bacons

translated by Holly P. Cuff, Teacher/Poet,
Fort Lee High School, New Jersey

GRASS STAIN

mistakenly
fell on weeds beside the road
then did you see the flower buds

unexpectedly
you heard their anxiety
fretting inside

deliberately
returned home alone so vague
and suffering that often

translated by Andrew Young, Police Officer,
South Nyack, New York

LOOKING AT THE FLOWER

gazing upon the flowers we grasp
the buds created by themselves
yet how do they bloom thus

rooted flowers small and tall
all opening at day's dawn
casting a hopeful glance to the sky

holding stamen high
follow the flower way
devote a whole day

translated by John Barnard, Referee NCAA Ice Hockey

CLIMB UP THE HIMALAYA

The Himalaya Mountain is not there
For just anybody's climbing up.

The moon comes back over the mountain
Every fortnight.

Stepping stones in the creek are also frozen by icy rain.

Slippery mountains, up and down.
Three or four waterfalls
Of Niagara
Are comforting you
Not to weep in this valley.

Don't take it easy,
This frozen icy sacred mountain.

Climbing needs prayers and meditation
At least for a fortnight
As a follower of Siddhartha.

Life is a journey of climbing up to the mystics of the snow mountain

And down.

translated by Yearn Hong Choi

PUSHING OFF

rockland lake
settled by geese from canada
huddled for the winter
sheltering from the cold

till the sky reopens
having long wings restored
with short december days
tossing many long nights

nourished by drops of water
missing nature's call home
for all living beings

translated by Alexander P. Neill, Edinburgh, Scotland

SIXTY-SIX

mastered only eating food

translated by Jas S. Yoo, President/CEO,
Hanmi Bank, California

POEMS BY HYOUNG O KIM

TAPPAN ZEE BRIDGE

depleting daily savings
envying moon's freedom
and releasing burdens
borrowing dragonfly's wing
could fly over the water

push off
as if knocking down wooden gate
going to sunchang jangkumok

by desecrating the clouds
the hills lost their way on the road and
the sea rapidly rushed onto the fields
with the high tides

our old vows still echo loud
where does the
rice wine ferment

translated by Young Il Kim, Screenwriter

TIME AND TIDE

you and i run as a stream
started from a sky mountain

followed by wind and cloud
may meet some eddies and bends

but still keep running
toward the ebb and flow

till i stand at your side
with few words but
only eyes on you for good

translated by Eric J. Tommasi, M&T Bank

POEMS BY HYOUNG O KIM

WROTE A CARD

mother

creatures living on the soil
look not the same

calling their mothers
all differently

separated a part of body for pain but
anxious to give more than you have

mother

today I spoke your name
and wrote a card

translated by Alan B. Colsey, MBA Program Director
St. Thomas Aquinas College, New York

48

Poems by Ven. Kim Kyongam

Ven. Kyoungam is a chief monk in the Borimsa Temple, Fairfax, Virginia. He is a poet and artist from Cheju Island.

WIND FROM THE MOUNTAIN

Mountain birds' song is poetry from the wind
Blowing from the high land to the low land.

One landscape painting is the Buddha's smile,
Showing his Love and Mercy to the masses.

Human language is making a scripture,
Guiding the masses who lost their way in the wilderness.

Leaving my heavy burden, ambition and anger to the low land,
My mind is flowing as a river toward the sea, as the wind.

MOTHER'S PRAYER

—for her children's successful college entrance exam

Mother's impatience on the mountain trail
And on the hill of the wind
With one doe of rice and one dozen of candles
Comes to pray in front of the Buddha's image.

Clean water in the creek
Flowing through the rocks and
Mountain pigeons
goo goo goo goo
Are greeting the mother's thirst.

Her mind is dedicated to Buddha,
Her eyes and ears are parts of the sermon hall.
See and hear the things with His wisdom!

Her love is burning like a candle
With the monk's invocation
In the sacred time and space.

Mother is taking the college entrance test
On behalf of her son and daughter.
Alas! What is she doing?

Winter Temple

At Magoksa

Snow-covered Magok Temple,
Dim candlelight flickering the main sanctuary,
Sound out of the wooden-bell with a clapper,
Dokdolulu.....
Clean wave of sound from the giant copper bell
Are all awakening the quietness of a silent temple.
When the monk repenting his regrettable things in life
Is coming down to the main sanctuary,
The snowflakes are dancing on the front yard.
Each and every snowflake
Purifying his polluted mind
Is making the temple
The snow-white bliss
In which naked trees are neat and beautiful.
Snow-covering mountain temple
Is converting every prayer's heart
As a snow flower.
Oh, this is the *kukrak*, *Sukkarais*.

Wind from the Mountain Temple

Wind from the mountain temple
is the wind of Mercy.
O, the wind of fragrance
from the Buddha's Image Hall!
One water-color brush stroke on rice paper is
the heart of a humble monk.
One stroke of black-ink brush calligraphy
is the scripture of Buddha's teaching.
The poetry/calligraphy/water color art work
is a reflection of the metaphor seeking the Truth.
O, the songs of mountain birds are
making a harmony with the monk's chanting.
Wind from the mountain temple
is washing the dirt from the *Sabha* life.

NEW YEAR'S PRAYER

New sun rises over the sea line,
Empties my vain dreams last night,
And shines over the lotus flower in my temple pond.
Morning dews disappear from the lotus leaf.

As new year starts from this new sun,
Let me renew my soul and body every morning with new sun.

NEW SPRING

Buddha's smile awakens the Spring woods in long sleep.
Crocus flower, first,
Cherry blossom, second,
Magnolia blossom, third,
Azalea blossom, fourth,
And dogwood blossom, fifth

...the festival is centered on April 8,
Buddha's birthday, April 8, is the peak of the Spring festival.

AUTUMN WIND

Autumn sky is hung blue
Over the cosmos flower field.

The woods changes its color to
Yellow, brown and red.

The earth is waiting for the falling leaves
To cover the earth.

There is no financial crisis
In this autumn.

LOVE

Sacrificing all you have,
Receiving as little as possible

Love is no more, no less.

Love is the first sunlight
Breaking the night's last darkness.

Love is the most beautiful flower
When you feel.
If you do not feel,
Then it is just wind passing by
Without anyone's notice.

TO VEN. KYOUNGAM
WRITTEN BY YEARN HONG CHOI

He shows some poems and Oriental watercolor art works
to the town people that he composed and painted in the temple
of high mountains.

I come to know that he was Joongkwang's art teacher
and a student of poetry and literature under the famed poet Gongcho
Oh Sang-soon in the 1950s and early 1960s,
and a political exile in the United States of America since early
1980s under then Korean military rule.

Then, he sold his art work and established his temple
in Fairfax, Virginia. In recent times, he conducted a prayer night for
the Virginia Tech victims in his temple.
He is a modern day monk who practices Buddha's teaching
in the Capital of the United States.

When returning to the temple,
I hear the sounds of waves and seagulls
From Seoguipo, Cheju Island, his home island.

But I see his screen well composed of spring, summer, autumn and
winter; and seasonal flowers, bamboo, pine trees, birds and rocks. I
also see the Ven. Kyoungam from his back.

58

Poems by June C. Baek

June C. Baek was born in North Korea. She is a graduate of Yonsei University in Seoul, Korea and Sam Houston University, Texas (MA degree). June worked as a health information manager in Pennsylvania.

DAVID, ON HIS BIRTHDAY

Today, he is 12, one grandson and October born
Changing colors of the tree leaves was beautiful
Autumn air was still as if someone would visit.
He was born in the second C-section
We waited so long for his arrival
A few months thereafter he was sent to daycare with Julia
His sister side-by-side

Learned to crawl backward on steps when we watched
9-11 smoking tower on the TV screen
His grandparents' hair stood at the scene
His morning happy & smile made his mom happy
Guiltless full-time and hard-working mom
At 3 he was a chatterbox of imaginary stories

He was an intense observer of a truck pouring cement mix
Water running under a sewer grid at neighbor's yard
Fun with fireman's hat and engineer's helmet
Liked Halloween's Spiderman outfit best and
Enthusiastic eater; "more" was his favorite word

At 5, Saturday morning he cried for "mommy, one more kissie"
When he was heading to the Korean culture class
At the school auditorium he stood up firm and straight and
Was attentive to the principal and teacher's instructions

He loved games, chess he taught his classmates, friends
Before class started
Wondered at parents hiding his Star War games
"My parents are playing a trick on me; if it shows up
I want to show you Stage II, Grandma!"

At 8, on the football field, he helped fasten Jimmy's chin band
And asked Jimmy's help fastening his band too
He, the Center, was yelling and the game started
At Claude Moore practice field and
His "Jets" team at Bill Allen Field

He was a dealmaker: "Today we go to my house and
Next we go to yours"
For 2 hours until his parents come home
"I am for Mom's Democratic Party; Julia is for Dad's Republican
Party so, we 4 Baeks play fair."

Reluctant to overseas travel
But accepted the Korea trip with Julia at 10
At General McArthur Park, Incheon
He read every engraved writing
Of war and victory of 1950 Incheon landing

He is a quick thinker in math, homework and reading many books
A basketball and flag football player
CCD classes crowded his evening schedule
His tall, slender jumps on the basketball court I see
Now, it is time to sit back and see him grow his inner self

Ready to move up to middle school
Leaving us grandparents and neighbors behind
His challenge to a new school, new area, new friends

On his 12th birthday I sent him a card:
"If you receive this, it is because you are fun, intelligent,
and handsome
Is it right?"

AIRPORT WAIT

After our flight from Waco to Dallas in 25 minutes,
We waited for 2 hours for another flight to Washington, D.C.
At the boarding area at Gate A39,
Restroom 50 yards away, he didn't come back to me.

Desk attendant told me to call the airline, paging,
"Mr. B., please come to A39."
No response; next I am on the emergency cart
Searching for 20 more minutes,
When I returned he was not there.

Ran to A38, a long and fair-haired attendant took
My plea: "Travel partner is lost."

She called Airport police.
A helmeted, uniformed lady on a scooter
Took description: "Baseball cap, plaid shirt, brown pants, sneakers."
Gave me confident words: "I'll find him; go and wait at A39."

Soon she returned: "I found him outside C terminal,
Now you have to check him in thru SECURITY with boarding pass."
I ran against time, I have only 30 minutes to boarding.
Lined up for CHECK-IN with Lost & Found partner,
Ran back to Gate A39.

My past experience has told me:
When I rode a Toyota minivan on the riverbed
To the road-less Kenyan field where acacia trees whistle,
When I fell into a snow hole at Back-Doo mountain top in May,
When Mongol Gobi desert flooded to dab paved road,
When monsoon hurricane toppled Jeju-Island,
        I believe in the Mystery of Faith.

FLY BACK TO NEST

I hovered around my son's house for 10 long years,
Not knowing fate's jealousy, visiting
Grandkids so dear and darling in sight, Jewel and Dew.
I grew blind in comfort of passing age.
Forgot many fallouts, saw proud sunny days only,
So sure I mend the East and the West

Until Lara exclaimed, "A gap" thereof
Wham! The blow was a waking-up call,
Waiting and crawling I did for 3 months
Hoping calm days soon to return.

Was it the jealous spirit of her deceased mother
Or her smiling Dad snooping her carefree days?
I don't believe a devil's trick, it's only passing ill
For parents are good-to-you ancestors, not false fear.

For humiliation, I murmur, "It could be worse," and
To my son's anger, I flew to my cocoon
And like a snow owl in a winter blizzard waited
Eyes blinked, took flying rather than to tears.

I found an escape back to my old nest, calling sick sister
I have a $1,500 ticket in my hand, my legs steady and sure
Back to where I flew away 50 years ago
Naked and cold I search for soft feathers, nest waits for me no more.

A view from the 17th floor, a Medical Center
Skyscrapers, vertical matchbox apartments many and far.
Mountain range in the north backdrops the city Seoul
On the banks of Han River blue stream, cars stream day and night.

Glare of silver and red jewels dotted night streets below.
No more my mother's white rubber shoes or her thatch roof below.

My sister sits on a hospital bed; in her I see my Mom,
I plead, "Just one more spoon, my dear sister."
My tears fell into soybean soup bowl for her.
She closes her eyes, lifts hand; can't take my feeding,
So tired, so frail and my agony set:
She was so strong, and cut-edge sharp-tongued once

Through 3 spoonfuls, she opened her eyes
To tell me, "Go home as soon as the next flight.
I will go home too after you go back
To your family and to your son; you belong there."
Though "Love" is all we have left to give;
And remember: "We girls are born to give man love."

She rubbed me of her Soul for the last.

Magic Key

Don't leave the apartment without a key,
A key message in her brain to keep.
She walked out to walk her two dogs
To the foggy, damp morning mist.
Wet leaves slid 10 legs; Sara's square chin,
Micky's tail dripping,
Leashed thru her basement door.

She felt a chainless key in her pocket,
Talking to herself, "This is not the one; I forgot
The chained key bunch on the kitchen counter!"
Back to outside for help,
Too early in the morning at 8 o'clock,
"Shall I call a locksmith?"
No cell phone in my pocket either.

After an embarrassing 60 minutes
At 9 Mario came pushing his yellow cart.
She handed him the same key from her pocket,
He thrusts it into the same hole, unopened,
Next, into another underneath, opened,
She stood there to watch him play magic
In awe.

Recovery

He collapsed at Homily in the packed church
Bystanders whispered "911," some "Ambulance"
Ushered to the lobby for fresh air
Before he sat on a sofa, ambulance blinked
Rescue Squad in front

Crew of 8; stretcher and monitor
One with writing pad for name and medicine
One dotted his chest to EKG wire
Octogenarian shoulder skin and bone
Once harnessed a 40-lb. Army backpack up the mountain
Oversized boots slid down the hill to the frozen river bed

Vital signs good, taken to ER for more tests
Treatment rooms wide open
MD, RN, NP, and TECH names on the board
Wall clock needled at 11:30
IV lines, BP hookups fastened to him
To white linen-draped, 4-wheeled bed

Anxious waiting for Dr.'s order: "When tests are negative
And you can walk the hallway straight, go home"
Blood, urine, CT to dizziness; sure to pass
For his spirit strong, body hangs on

Symptoms "Near Syncope" reached
Superb coordination, warm service
Runs like a business store
No fear of a cliff to be pushed to

Beyond materials and teaching of faith
Unexplained humanity in the air
People respect people engrained
In this culture of the land we live

My heart swells with happy recovery
From love of neighbors, sure helping hands
To walk under a warm sunny sky
To golden scarlet leaves of Virginia tree

BACK FROM BOSTON

*(Watching this week's news of the Boston Marathon bombing, 4-15-2013;
revision of "Back from Boston," a memoir)*

Too many cars, so many lights, stopped me for 4 miles
To the daycare door
Faltering, I hold a sheet of paper to sign and
Take him to a pediatrician for aftercare
He had fallen from playground jungle gym

More wait for a doctor; through a window blind
I see a yellow belly baby duck
Making waves across the pond
As I made many waves of destiny

He has a 2-inch Band-Aid on his spotless forehead
His curled dark hair behind ear dips, exactly like his Dad
He is four years old; his Dad was two when he fell from 3rd floor window;
I was too eager for more income
Leaving precious time for my growing son
To my mom who does her way
She valued chores, meticulous folds
I woke up to a priority of duty
Shook the dust from my feet and left Boston

Less is more than more Bostonians have
Their houses creak and crack in the long winter
More learned complaints
More time to drink in the bars facing the church
Happier are the working people in Pennsylvania where
Busy hands and quiet prayers are valued in the town
Mothers cook meatballs, and she makes salads
Fills the neighborhood with yummy smells
From this corner to the end of row houses

Where mothers yell, drive kids to school,
Mother's help, help everywhere
Fussing kids in the morning: "Take jackets with you,"
She has sheets on the line in the backyard to fold later
Chase kids out while she vacuums,
Spring cleaning of bay window, sweep winter salt from driveway
While she is on his disability check
Mom's home-cooked meal is on the plate
Dinnertime for four, all eating the same food like we used to

Mom and Dad, full-time professionals these days
Too busy to eat with or think family
The kitchen gleams clean and bouquet of roses on the island
Food ordered by cell phone
Cold pizza on kid's lap, sit in front of TV
A family dog watches him eat
Cats lick their meals in the kitchen corner; and
Noise, noise everywhere, but not a voice to hear

When I woke up from this daydream
The doctor opened his Band-Aid
"Take this off at bedtime; it will heal in no time"
In two days his parents return home from their anniversary vacation
I am not in Boston, not in Pennsylvania, now in Virginia
That Thursday he doesn't want to go to daycare, and I insist, "Do not skip"
It was a lucky day, when child-god guarded him
I watch the news all day, far, far away
Back from the Boston bombing

STITCHING STATION AND SEN NING BARI*

One long and boring summer day I stumbled in front of a store
I saw the store full of caps, shirts, and children's clothes with names, logos
One computerized sewing machine for logos on caps and hats
One for the straight stitches, names and badges on a flat surface
The Yoko sewing machine, proud 200 years of history; an art form

I took a fancy of day-dream, of years ago summer
When I saw three grievous mothers on the street corner
To beg Sen Nin Bari from us girls coming home from school
"Please give one stitch for my son to go on mission, Dok Ko Tai"**
To a Kamikaze flight to smash an enemy ship in the Pacific War

Thousand stitches she needs to make one vest
Did it protect him, or was it a myth she desperately needed?
She did not protest "War" but mourning tears in her heart
Warmonger Samurai leaders took her preciously raised son at 19
After two months training in the ice water to a solo, suicide flight

At the stitching station I see shelf full of Nationals baseball team
Red cap with "W" letter in black stitch, a soaring new club
It sells like a hotcake to the owner's pride
Beauty of embroidery remained today
In the business world of computer proficient products.

*Japanese words, thousand stitches
**Japanese words, solo flight

70

TAME ON TIME

When he was 9 his Dad told him, "If you
Don't, I have to take your game time away, go to
CCD class tonight with your sister"
He did; not her at 13, too late for her, her Dad thought

When he was 8 his Dad said, "We go to look
For your lost glasses," and took him to the school gym
Where he played one night before, then to the classroom where
The night cleaner opened the door
His mother had gone out of town for a business trip

When his two kids were 12 and 10, I took them for an education trip
To Jeju Island, Korea, for the wonder of volcanic craters and
   women divers
A monsoon storm in August fast and fierce
Delayed their return flight inland for hours
Anxious tourists crowded the airport waiting room
Push and shove for every flight cancelled

Two kids unaware of the storm warning in Korean
Giggle in their comic books
Scared, I plead, "You brought me here
Help me take them back to their mother
They are hers, not even mine!"

"Please come first in the line with your two children,"
An attendant from the boarding desk yelled to me
You say a miracle, faith, or a prayer answered, we
Got out of the stormy island on the last flight
Their Dad whispered to me: "Just enjoy the kids, Mom,
We are the ones who raise them"

TIME OUT

On the way to visit Jackie's store in Greenwich Village, New York
My car spun 180 degrees, hitting the curve
Stopping head up the hill
200 meters short of the stop light
To the Holland Tunnel.

I danced with proud ego, making it in 4 hours from Washington, D.C.
Before the tunnel was clogged for hours
Joys took over, blinding me to the sign "Slow"
At the sharp curve, down the hill on a foggy day
Car flew on the breaks at 60 miles an hour.

Steering wheel wacky, front tire flat
Yet I walked out scratch-free
In front of a gas station where
New York bums swamped and squatted on the steps
One asked, "Do you have a spare tire?"

His tool use fast and exact
My "thank you" and tip sincere
The priceless homeless I see
They are there to give a hand for anybody, anytime,
Angels without feathers, sit there for TIME OUT.

RICH AND POOR

Three cousins met in Palm Springs, California, where
My rich cousin spent winters to escape from rainy Seattle and
Another cousin helped with daily chores: cooking, driving, and
Shopping after her divorce, I was the third cousin

We were from the same family 3 generations ago
From a patriarchal, hardworking, conservative and common
Korean culture of farming millets, potatoes, soybeans
We left the village at once when the Korean War broke out in 1950

Many years since then separated us from Korean refugee camp to
Seattle; Salem, Oregon and Washington, D.C.
One rich capitalist in the real estate business in Seattle and
The other two reminiscing about our parents, laughed and cried

We sat in front of home-cooked rice and soup
Dinner was plain; Kimchi was a major staple
Talk was longer, and
We remembered G-G parent's farmland vividly

One lost her Mom at 6 in the refugee camp, coldest winter,
Christian God stretched his strong arms to her
Her brother, a preacher, professor, a prolific writer, was a rock in
Her family, they loved each other

My rich cousin married young in order to lessen the family burden
Made a living while sitting at a yarn store knitting, selling for 20 years
Finally earned 15%, 20% profit to buy, buy land
Land will not go to waste and be lost
Nobody knows how much she would be worth
"Making money is my hobby!" she claimed

She banged, "I don't speak English" to a call from her son's girlfriend
I believed in the American "melting pot" and became a "lawful citizen" in
10 years. She calculates what mortgage notes yield and
Her travel plans included a trip to Jeju Island to build a new condo
And Hawaii for Hampton Inn, a chain business

On Sunday morning two cousins sang hymns in the kitchen
Rich cousin was frugal, plain in lifestyle, stays away from rich people
But she liked Palm Springs' sun and desert
Both did not see Angel's trumpet, palm trees, or snow mountain surrounding

She points to a red brick building near the foot of the mountain on
My way to the airport, she loved swimming in an open-air mineral
Hot spring twice a week, "To relieve my chest congestion," she said
Coughing too deep, January air could be dry-cold in this area

Back to the native land, the story exhausted us all
She confessed, "I learned business from your father!" who was
The first businessman in our clan, but my father could not make money
I wished the rich cousin would keep her savvy skills

Farewell to my rich cousin; with her pride, now she says,
"English is my language"
And learns American laws and regulations, manners and business ethics
To stay afloat as a big fish in the ocean and to be a
World-class citizen

POEMS BY HOGILL KIM

Poet, Korean Airline Pilot, Korea Daily reporter and cultural editor; most recently a farmer in the Mexican desert. He is known as a famed Sijo poet in Korea and in the United States of America. He has several collections of poems in Korean. *Desert Poems*, his poetry book in English translation will be published soon.

DESERT POEM

—MONARCH BUTTERFLY

Why do they come down and up
Over several thousand kilometers?
Where is their hometown and destination?
Well, whenever they are resting,
Those places must be their hometown.

Don't ask me why they travel.
What does it mean to butterfly?
They just fly over the distance
With their fragile life as a warranty.

Passing time under their wings,
Passing the Earth under their wings,
Are life and death the basic instinct?
Mystery of sky
Drawn by their body
Is there over the distance.

DESERT POEM

—RATTLESNAKE

Standing up your body,
That is your pride.

The sound of a bell
Always awakens your soul.

You alone manage your life
With a poisonous pocket
In your body.

DESERT POEM
—HUMMINGBIRD

Is it difficult to sustain your body?
Flying as hard as a thunderstorm,
You maintain your life.
Standing still,
Standing still,
Oh, beautiful moments!

Desert Poem
—I will be 70 the day after tomorrow

After passing 60,
I still do not know when I will pass away
As if frosted wild chrysanthemum.
I will be 70
On the day after tomorrow.
The sound of a bell
As if it is a sharp knife,
Please wake me up,
The soul of the bell.

DESERT POEM

—IF YOUR SORROW IS TOO BIG

If sorrow is too big,
No more tears.
Tears are luxurious to the soul,
When you can depend on something.
Hope is the only thing you can depend on.
Often hope is not there,
Only despair is there to depend on.
No water drops in the desert.

Desert Poem

—Louis Vuitton

Recently, fakes are better looking than the real ones.
I don't know whether my poems are going to be classified
As the fakes or the real things.

DESERT POEM
—PALM TREE

New young leaves are green
Above and over the brown leaves dying.
Standing tiptoe
Inch by inch,
Dancing over the dead leaves.
Life and growth.

DESERT POEM
—METEOR

I am a man in a star existing far away
a billion light-years
From the home country,
A stranger in foreign countries,
Always dreaming to leave for another unknown star sooner
Or later.

DESERT POEM

—LIKE A PALM TREE

He was an outsider forever.
He did not scram with you.
Possessing always clean purity, absolute solitude,
Like a palm tree,
He stood against the darkened twilight.
Then, he became a star shining in the night sky.

DESERT POEM

——FOR A CAMEL

Two eyes are the twin lakes of sorrow.
Walking the burning desert and sand hills
With one hump or two.

Yellow dust winds
From time to time
Threaten your move,
But you move one step to another
Looking for an oasis after a brilliant constellation of stars.

When words of prayers are wrapped in the sunset,
You are standing there forever.
I see the permanent image of camel,
Which shall never perish.

POEMS BY SE WOONG RO

Se Woong Ro is a poet and essayist. He worked for the Korean Foreign Ministry and the World Bank. Se was the former president of the Yoon Dong-ju Memorial Group-Washington Chapter. He has one poetry book, *The Wayfarer of Kilimanjaro*, (in Korean) in 2012.

GIFT CERTIFICATE

My volunteer teaching job was compensated by a Korean grocery
store's gift certificate—it was a bag of rice.
My only job after retirement was volunteer teaching
at the Korean Senior Center.
So far I have been compensated by my own satisfaction
helping senior citizens learn computer skills.
Their learning about word-processing and emailing messages to
their grandchildren has made them enormously happy.
I taught and treated my students as post-doc program students
at the Korean Senior Center.
My wife smiled when I presented a gift certificate to her —
a bag of rice.

Poet

A life-long poet could not buy his own apartment
with all the payments from his creative writing,
but he could be a millionaire,
an emperor, a magician,
living in a mansion and in a palace.
He could fly over the Pacific Ocean
to reach his hometown
in the blinking of a moment.
He could be a flying Tarzan in the African jungle
if and when he desired.
He has been and will be a dreamer in his poetry
or in his poverty.
Poetry is very close to poverty in spelling.
Well, I have a dream, too.

FALLEN LEAF

Don't say,
"You are beautiful!"
I did not want to fall onto the ground.
I wanted to remain on the branch where I belonged.
In the summer,
I hid the birds' nest with my green clothes
from the predator's invasion.
I protected the nest from rain, wind and storm.
I enjoyed the musical all the birds were orchestrating
in the woods.
But I had to accept my fate to fall onto the ground
in autumn.
But I did not want to fall.
Therefore, don't tell me, "You are beautiful!"

KILIMANJARO

I want to go to Kilimanjaro again.
I prefer Kilimanjaro
to Paris, London, Moscow, and New York.
Rough and tough journey to Nairobi, Kenya and a four-hour
drive on the road paved and unpaved to Kilimanjaro.
It was often more than a four-hours drive because
the tire went flat in the wilderness or we had a mechanical failure.
In the morning, I sip coffee with monkeys.
We were watched by the wild animals;
elephants, giraffe, tigers, leopards, wildebeast...
they are the owners of Africa and
we are only visitors.

AT THE BARBER SHOP

A senior citizen with a cane and
with a wife walked into the old barber shop.
His wife helped him sit on the seat.
His medal honoring his military career
was shiny on his chest.
A Vietnamese barber greeted him: "Long time, no see."
His response: "How are you?"
Their chats covered American politics to
American economy — all down turned.
Their conclusion was — all gloomy.
The barber shaved his face and massaged his back.
Extra service with friendship, no charge.
The old couple left the shop and walked down the hill
slowly, holding hands together.
After they left, I sat down on the seat he left
and closed my eyes.

A MAPLE EXCURSION

More than 50 years have gone like wind
since we graduated from high school in Seoul, Korea.
Those who have survived and succeeded on their journeys
got together at a Texas lakeside resort.
Reunion with name tag on the chest made them all
high school students.
They tried to remember old names, young faces and
innocent smiles.

Maple trees were all red at the lakeside resort.
Their reunion was the maple excursion,
beautiful red as ever.

MEALS ON WHEELS

A Korean old man and woman are waiting for the hot meals on wheels.
Rainy day, stormy day, snowing day, hurricane day.
I volunteered to deliver the Korean meals daily from the church
kitchen to their nursing home.
I knocked on the door, no response.
After a long wait, the old woman opened the door and greeted me:
"You are my savior; you are my life saver; you are my angel."
Meals on wheels are heaven.
Her wheelchair was broken, so she crawled from her room to the door.
It was a long journey.

Black-White Picture

Inside the farm house,
one black and white picture hung so long
on the wall.
After mother passed away,
I brought that picture and placed it in my study
at my house in Virginia.
My granddaughter was curious about that picture
and asked me who that was in the picture.
I asked her to guess who it was.
She could not figure out that boy
in a middle school uniform and cap in the 1950s.
Finally she asked me:
Which star did that boy come from?

I smile at the picture and at my precious granddaughter.
Precious beyond all things.

SNOWY NIGHT

Deep Night
Telephone ringing:
who can that be?
Outside the window,
heavy snowflakes are falling.
Someone could not sleep in the snowing night.
Who is calling me?
She may be, or may not be.
Snowing outside.

Guess who?
inside.

MOONKYUNG HILL

Heavy snow falling and filling the deep
valley of the Moonkyung Hill.
No way of finding the road.
Snow covered the hills and valleys.
Bus was stuck in the snow.
Passengers came out of the bus,
walking down the hill like crabs.
Layered reeds in silver clothes
were weeping in the darkness.
Light in the village at the foot of the hill
comforted the wayfarers.
Who would be waiting for the wayfarers
all night
in the village?

Poems by Sung Ho Lee

Sung Ho Lee is a poet and novelist in California. She has a
couple of poetry books, *California Reed* and *Why I am afraid of
Myself* (both in Korean). She has two novels, *Ninety Nine Steps*
and *Yellow Ribbon at the Pyongyang Railroad Station* (both in Ko-
rean). She has a collection of short stories, three collections
of essays, and one biography.

CALIFORNIA REEDS

Crammed together we live, 'tho,
All the rubbing and bumping brings no warmth,
Only emptiness.
I wave my soul to the sky and plead,
Yet the rivers and hills of yesterday refuse to fade;
Reed flower tosses itself airborne
Only to sail into the wind-wall, nostalgia.

Destitute wind brings
Recorder tunes;
Sound that beckons me.
Yesterday at the village creek
Sank my teeth into slender reeds
And at night I rolled down
The hills of azalea blossom, didn't I.

At the end of the Pacific
I edge over the blue-rock cliff,
Mang Bu Sok,
a woman who becomes a stone statue
while waiting for her husband,
I crane my neck
And await the news from
The violet world.

Crammed together we live, 'tho,
I yearn for home more every day,
I lean and edge closer to my neighbor
Only to see the stranger turn away.
Reed flower tosses itself airborne
Only to sail into the wind-wall, nostalgia.

WINTER TREE

At last
You have no more to shed
Now in your white vein,
All over,
Remain only cold blue pulses.
Never looking back
At those who left:
Long hands of divine nature.
Empty hands point to sky
In silence, mutter,
The prayers of the winter tree.

SCULPTURE EXHIBIT

Statues groan, oppress
Exhibit hall space

A statue labeled "Mommy"
Stands forlorn

Withstood for years
Wind, rain
Till it transformed
From a plain rock
To a mother sculpture,
Now a crumbling shell

As long as she lives she says
She must give more
Prays on her knees at dawn
Teary prayers
For her children

Countless chiseling.
Sculpture hammer's
Effort
Notwithstanding
The Mommy statue
Stands mute

Mom's Cellular Phone

Waiting has been her life,
Waiting has been her fate,
Waiting has been her mission.
It has been out to her hands from her heart
In modern times.

In her young wife's time,
She waited for her husband's homecoming from an exile
In China for the national independence from Japanese yoke or his letters
Every day and night.

Now, she is waiting for her children's homecoming or calls.
Her telephone is in her hands.
She is waiting for her seven children's calling every day.

She is a 95-year old mother,
Still waiting for her children's good news.
No! Her mission is waiting for just calls from each child.
No news is no longer good news.
Children, please call your mom every day at least once.

MOM'S WEATHER MAP

Sinewy hands of my sons
Carved English alphabets on jade stone;
I try to scratch Korean letters
With rusty plane on soft wood

Bittersweet old and new country,
Children's fast paced thoughts,
I discarded more than just
My fingertips, it seems

Tiny tots on my back,
I left my hometown,
Thatched house
To build new rainbows on this land

One day,
Two days passed,
Regret soared in me,
A rising balloon in the sky,
I looked up and saw the sun
Hidden behind clouds

Oh, children, my sons,
Draw me a smiling sun
For my weather map tomorrow

EMPTY NEST

No permission granted, a dove pair
Built a nest
Over the porch, laid eggs,
Hence, the birds ruled the roost,
And I, a humble boarder
In my own home,
Minding my footsteps, lest
I disturb the babies in waiting

The day my son left home
For the world of his own, the birds flew away, too

Carefully, I nudge open
The porch door at dusk
For a peak at the doves
Empty, I stare at the nest
I go to my son's room,
Turn on the light,
Run my hand over his desk,
His hand prints still fresh to my touch

One stormy night last winter
I heard in the rain a voice
"Umma—" then
A ring on the telephone,
The news of the accident
That night, too, I stared at
The empty nest,
Called out his name
Under my breath

Neckar River

Ancient midnight
Bells ring time past,
Mountain fog chases wind,
The sunset, over
Heidelberg castle
Standing naked,
Bathing in the ringing toll,
Shy of this visitor.

Dark past dissolved,
Massive castle floating,
Tears from young Berter,
The Prince's love melted
To the river's floor,
Where all the thoughts layered
The mighty river water.
I walk down the river bank
Hands clasped in back and
Look behind, I see
In the river no sadness,
Nothing merry in particular.

Neckar bridge pretends
To know nothing even though
It must know everything
From this bank to the other,
Between every stone block
Moss holds rainwater.
The glasses held in toast glitter
The moonlight as it flows.

No matter how many years
It doesn't age;
'tho night is old
It doesn't sleep, the river.
A fleeting vagabond,
I live for a thousand years and
I drift on.

SPRING RAIN

First day, tickling
Second day, getting wet
Third day, socking completely
Like the first love

Desert defies to be a desert,
Combing all day
Wet hair

New green pine trees are decorated by crystal dew flowers,
Yearning, heavier on my eyebrows

Secret

You are a high mountain
Hidden by thick fog

Autumn rain is falling
On mountain over mountain

I climb up mountain,
Calling your name

Goldmine is not exposed to the foggy mountain,
But you are my goldmine in my heart

You are my mountain fortress
Hidden by fog

You are my permanent shelter
Protected by so many shields

Cup of Tea

Don't tell me it is just small.
The cup of tea is a small object,
But contains many good thoughts with the tea,
Reflecting so many good friends sharing so many good memories.
Even sorrowful moments in the past turn out as beautiful ones
Inside the recollection.
Tears and laughs are all inside the cup.
Oh, our eyes seeing each other with a cup of tea in our hands
exchange more poetic messages
than the sounds of toast, cheers and clicks of wine glasses.
When my friends are out of my sight,
They will remain with me
Whenever I sip a cup of tea.

Don't tell me it is just small.
Oh, it is a lovely object in my daily life.

POEMS BY YEARN HONG CHOI

Yearn Hong Choi—A prolific and distinguished writer who has won awards in Korea and the US with six books of poetry and one collection of short stories. His essays and short stories appeared in prestigious journals such as *Short Story International* and *World Literature Today*. In 1994, he became the first poet from Korea to be invited to read at the Library of Congress; Pulitzer Prize-winning writer Gwendolyn Brooks introduced Choi by reading a poem she wrote about him.

To Doctor P

The deer I meet on the trail has two beautiful eyes.
Where does he go to have his glasses?

Ben Franklin invented the glasses for me.
Why didn't he invent a pair of glasses for the deer?

Doctor P: I have never received such a question in my life.

KITCHEN

The time is always summer;
A Korean couple has immigrated to a nation on the equator,
Playing with fire.
Or they are working next to the fire.

Even with winter cold outside
Summer is always inside;
Oil is burning
And meat is roasting at medium rare or well done.
Their hands are burned by fire and oil,
And their fingers are cut by a knife.

The hungry patrons are not always courteous to them.
The couple plays music to their patron's level of hunger.
They place steak and potatoes neatly on their plate,
And salads in the bowl on the table.
They become the purgatorial saints.

When the moon rises in the mid-sky,
The couple is heading to their nest
Where their children had already left for college.
They fall into sleep without time to make love.

Every night they have a dream together
To return to their home country.

Poet's Daughter

Poet's daughter brought a gift of five pebbles
From her Ireland trip to her father.

It was the best gift to her inland dad
Who sees the beauty in the pebbles formed from the crashing waves
on the sea shore.

The pebbles are losing the seawater in his study,
But they will be good companions to the poet
Who comforts his sea fever.

Anyway, they are the expression of daughter's love of her dad.

112

ODE TO SLEEP

a suckling babe fell asleep on mom's breast
a sleeping grandson slumped next to grandpa
a poet dozing off held in lover's arms
a dude falling asleep in barber's chair
a migrant worker snoring in the bouncing truck on a country road
tired out soldiers dead asleep oblivious of shellfires and smoke
peace, deep peace is birthed inside abyss of sleep
within repose are gentle waves and sea birds of home port
beyond the scent of pines stretches the sleepy sandy beach

Oklahoma, Oklahoma

1

Full physics gone grotesque is more surreal than A-bomb.
The alchemy of cold and warm, moist and dry air further chilled
already shivering incongruity that its disharmonious harmony
could be exploded in the cradles of sleeping babies.
Just to prove the presence of indomitable metaphysics
exceeding the deadly physics of E=MC2?
The theory goes some things are irrelevant
with respect to the theory of high science, ugh,
some calls it the dark side of Nature subjected to frustration,
however, not by its own choice.
(from the Fragment From An Unpublished Dialogue of Dionysus)
Cyclones shredding human body, soul and spirit
at the speed exceeding the velocity of the darkest light —
who could comprehend this really surreal physics?
Who could have known this nonsense apart from the Book of Black Holes?
We do have too many holes in all our theories.

2

Cold, dry air from the north confronted hot, moist air from the south.
The confrontation made a powerful wind,
200 miles per hour,
That destroyed a peaceful town in Oklahoma in a few minutes
Like an atomic bomb did.
As a giant man rooted out a tall tree,
The cyclone rooted out the town and turned it upside down.
Real houses and cars were flattened like toy houses,
And toy cars.
I could not believe what I saw on the television screen.

In the background of the ruins,
I saw a sign, God bless Moore, in a strange war zone.
Did God bless Moore?
Does God bless Moore?
Seven young, innocent children were killed in an elementary school.
Several adults were killed in 20 minutes warning.
God blessed the survivors of some 40,000 residents and lifted the
  dead to heaven.
That was a Miracle.
He has already built a bridge from Earth to Heaven with a new hope
  and dream.
God bless Moore.
God loves Moore, More.

PRAYER

A couple of doves came out of mother's embroidery work and flew.
Mature adults and young children put their two hands together,
Kneeling on the floor,
And whispered their words to God.
Then, the words spread out to the sky
As the doves spread out their wings.
The words are making music to heaven:
vibration of violin strings and piano keys.
Tears from their eyes are covering the minor scale to the major scale
In the music to heaven.

PRAYING HANDS

—to Albrecht Durer

Yearning, suffering, hope and aspiration.
Silent language from the soul's ascent to heaven:
The mother prays for her son living in a foreign land
every dawn with a bowl of fresh water from the spring.

A man's hard labor in the mines has financed his brother
who has become a success as a young artist.
The bones in every thin finger have been smashed and abused
with suffering arthritis. He cannot paint with his damaged hands.

A candle is burning next to his two hands fused in one.
A blessing descends to the darkened room lit by the candle.

A young woman dreams to swim across the ocean
inside her lover's prayers to reach the other side of the ocean
every morning.

Our world of blissfulness!

In the morning of Chusok *

A box of carrot cake baked with walnuts
Was delivered to my front porch
In the early morning hours of Chusok.
Oh, newly harvested apples and pears
Were also placed beside the box of cake.
The mailman could not yet deliver them
In that early hour.
Only an angel could come to my house with a gift from heaven
Dewed with fading moon- and star-light
In that hour.
My Thanksgiving ceremonial breakfast table was full and more thankful.
What a blessing!
Thank you, my angel.

*Chusok is Korean Thanksgiving

GOODBYE TO MY UNCLE
—at his cemetery in San Francisco

You have been a romanticist, never getting old even in the last
  moment of your life.
You have overcome a language barrier, racial and ethnic discrimination
in Japan and the USA as a young boy and a mature adult.

You have been courageous in overcoming all the difficulties of life set
in a poverty-stricken farm village in Korea and post-War Japan, and
an affluent society in San Francisco.

In the midst of a difficult life, you always saw the beauty of life, using
oil and Oriental watercolor to draw your childhood farm house, and
later to draw the Bay area landscape or photographing beautiful moments.

You failed to treat your diabetes and instead drank hard liquor over
the years. You travelled to Korea, Japan and the world with a never
fading youth and romanticism. You had a young heart throughout
your life. "How many speeding tickets did you receive, my uncle?"
"Many," you answered.

You were damn proud of the Choi family from North Choongchung
Province in Korea.

In May 1968, you forced me to get off the cruise ship, American
President, anchored in Yokohama, Japan which was heading to San
Francisco via Honolulu and come to your house in Chiba, Japan by a
taxicab. Then, you bought me a Northwest Airline ticket from Tokyo
to Seattle. "You are the first Choi studying in the United States, I
cannot let you sail to San Francisco. You must take a flight."

That was the way I landed in Seattle, USA. You then followed me. You
finally established Edoya, the jewelry store that took up one entire

block of downtown San Francisco. You built a fortune and took me to
Reno, Nevada one weekend to find and enjoy another world of the
USA. You were brave to lose big and win big in Reno. That was you.

Your wife, my aunt, answered my question, "Why did you marry my
uncle?" Her answer was simple, "He is the manliest man I have ever met."

My wife whispered to me when you entered my Virginia home for
the first time," Your uncle looks like a prominent university
president." You smiled at my wife.

You have been ambitious and hopeful. You have been a tearful man
with compassion and loving care.

I will miss you forever.

San Francisco has been you, and will be so forever,
As Chiba, Japan has been you and will be so forever to me.

God bless you.
You have been my one and only uncle in the USA and will be so forever.
My uncle, Choi Hyoo Hyoung or Edward Kawana

120

HOT MEALS ON WHEELS

Those who cook rice and soup,
Those who transport hot meals to the nursing home, and
Those who eat hot meals and soup delivered.
They are three different bodies, but one body.

Those who make pizza in the kitchen,
Those who deliver the pizza to the consumers, and
Those who eat the pizza delivered.
They are three different bodies, but not necessarily one.

The groups may be the same,
But they are quite different.

The former is the volunteers for those old handicapped men and women
Who cannot cook by themselves.
The latter is the market economy for money
Between the businessmen and the consumers.

One group is in the Holy Communion.
The other group is in the business in action.

10 years holy communion
Of hot meals on wheels
Are just great
As much as the silent river flowing from the highland to
The sea.

POEMS BY YOUN SEOK SEO

Dr. Youn Seok Seo is a surgeon retired from his long
medical practice in Ohio. He made his literary debut via
the Poetry Monthly in Korea. He has published one poetry
book, *Gracious Maria* (in Korean) and one book of essays,
Hello Dr. Seo (in Korean).

GRACIOUS MARIA

There is a head of a girl on the bookshelf in the clinic.
I see Maria Gonzales, a girl who probably lived
in a remote mountain village of Mexico.
When we touch her imaginary soft face,
we feel the holes,
where the twelve nerve fibers went through,
where the red pulsating arteries and the blue veins
passed through.

When we draw a line on her temple with a black ball point pen,
we are staring at the stern eyes of the juries
as they were making the verdict of bone fracture.
Whoever has questions, whoever studies medicine,
all come to see Maria.

Through the absolute silence of her head,
we hear the murmuring of clear water,
we see the colorful rainbows,
we taste and smell the delicious food.
Homo sapiens who can imagine, think, write, use
the hands, create, and teach others,
we see ourselves through her head.

In her, we see a cadaver in the anatomy lab with
its piercing odor of formalin tearing our eyes.
Here is the vestige of the soul,
the dead body whose skin has been torn, dissected
revealing reddish muscle, white yellowish nerve fibers,
whose bone cut into pieces and the internal organs exposed.

Sixteen-year-old virgin girl, Maria,
you will always preside over us

on the top of the bookshelf in the clinic,
shrouded in your perpetual youth.
Whenever we call, you will descend to us to be
the shining light in the darkness.

Oh, lovely Maria, you will live for thousands and
thousands of years in your own exalted place.

Heavenly Place

Hello there, my friend!
I came to the heavenly place I have only heard of.
Riding on a lovely rainbow, I happened to have
drifted here.
To this lofty place where the thick white clouds
form the vast ocean I reached after a long stretch of my arms.

In this land, under the blue sky, there are only
beautiful mountains.
Beyond them, endless mountain ridges, while
gentle hills undulate.
In this land, you hear no laboring sound of
waves nor the wailing of the winds, only the calm
blue sky.

Morning brings bright sunlight that dazzles our eyes.
The friendly neighbors greet one another during daytime;
in the evening we gather to bid farewell to the setting sun;
as night approaches, we seek the
tranquil haven for our soul.

After a long stretch, my friend, I followed smiling
children of the land with neither winter cold nor summer heat.
It is a land that is lightly sprinkled with rain and
where gentle breezes caress our faces, the land where we find
comfort and coolness in shadows of the palm trees.
It is the land that I have longed for.

Hello, my dear friend!
I have reached the heavenly place that I have only heard of.
Letting go of all, with empty hands,
climbing the colorful bridge,

purple to red, red to purple,
riding on the double rainbow, I came up to this
heavenly land.
Dear friend!

JOY OF SPRING

As I rushed out to see where the startled cry came from,
I was greeted by one purple flower leaf that has
just thrust its head through the melting snow.

From the branches of the trees, from all joints to
the finger tips that defied the harsh winter chill all through the wind
with their arms stretched.
Look, how those newborn buds are bursting out!

Last night's unseasonable thunderstorm summoned
armies of earthworms on the pavement oozing their smell.
The entire woods are clamorous with the endless
tales by the countless birds that have been silenced until
now. Again, spring has returned.

The golden bells offer their yellow flowers first;
azaleas dip the whole hillside in pink;
young people couple together;
while the opulent magnolia fragrance overflows
the yard.

Welcoming this season when the warm breeze
stealthily brush past the field, cradled in dense fog,
let us enjoy the spring day like those youthful pairs
dreaming of the blue sky with a rainbow.
After a long peaceful sleep in the nest,
when the dawn breaks,
let us fly away like the birds of passage.

LIMA LAND
—"Lima Land" the home of the Shawnee Indians
until their extinction.

Return of the spring rushes the melting ice to
the Ottawa River tributary that flows into the Great Lakes.

On the other side of the endless field, when the
dense fog is lifted, we can espy the thin thread of the long
Mississippi River; to every direction from the field,
we see the blossoming of new lives on this rich land.

This fertile land, ever drenched with the sweat of
the people who work from dawn till night,
has always yielded rich harvest of many grains;
even on the arid old oil field, they seeded green grasses.

In the woods over the corn and bean fields,
rabbits, squirrels and deer keep their homes and live happily along
with the luxuriant buckeye trees that offer a resting place for the
birds of passage, accompanied by the songs of wind and stream.

This is the land that has embraced countless lives
with unbound generosity.

Time flows on this land, the homeland, for a
handful of people who had to communicate with their
gesture because of their foreign tongue. Here in Lima Land, people
come and go, live and die; after releasing their soul,
their bodies return to the handful of soil at Woodlawn Cemetery
where they rest in eternal sleep, in silence.

Each year the names of the departed increase in number;
only the birds in the trees respond to them by their songs;
on each subsequent tombstone,
the long, mournful shadows of the setting sun linger.

Among the names of the people who perpetuate
their long lineage, name such as Shin, Kim, Lee
modestly raise their heads,
those who are far from the different shore
and built a small village on one corner of the land.
"Seoul Brothers" who lived in a tight knit, small
enclave, have drifted along with the half-century of tide,
the tireless tide that gradually erased their faces
and obliterated memories of them.
I wonder and ask myself:
Have the departed left any footprint on this Lima Land?

Dear friend,
after we are gone, life in this land will go on,
new people with unfamiliar clothes and music
will come to this land.

Dear friend, we who ride on the floating clouds,
when the sun is lost beyond the horizon,
in this vast universe,

let us now find the sign of our lonely twin planet
that is beckoning us, wandering in solitude,
somewhere from the thousands light years away.

In Lima Land,
through the clear sky,
let the rushing light from the stars
shower on this peaceful field.
Here in Lima Land, the night sky is pristine and lofty.
We can descry even the dark space
amidst the Milky Way endlessly
turning where the magnetic waves pass
as fast as light speed.

Oh, dear friend, let this be our plea!

Lima Land! Cherish our memories and let them
dwell in the deep heart of the land, forever.
Let no tides of time carry and
swallow them into the dark abyss of oblivion.

ON VISITING SIRE'S GRAVE

Once more, he has endured a long, cold winter
shrouded by heavy snow, under the chilly stars.
Over the crag, when I visit the grave, lifting heavy sod,
he greets me: "You have come a long way!"

Annoyed by the unwieldy yellow flowers that spread a thick banquet
Over the mound, I began pulling and weeding them,
until I hear Sire's voice: "They are fine; let them be,"
smiling through the yellow flowers.

Innumerable spirits must be whirling on the moist hill,
from every tree branch stretched, I hear the baby birds,
singing the song of the new land.

Caressed by the softly dancing spring breeze,
the entire hill is gradually dyed in light green.
By the clear stream where I dip my hand,
I hear his voice through the gushing stream:
"To you, the creator and the protector of the world...."
His voice in prayer is pounding my heart.

OUR FATHER WHO NEVER FAILED TO RETURN

Under the dimly lit moonlight, do you remember,
dear brother,
we used to wait for father who waded through
the rice paddy,
after the village market day was over?

Past the tall poplar tree by Sung-man's house,
following the winding path where the vociferous
frogs' chorus greeted us, holding up the lamp, holding
older sister's hands.
The night path where we used to wait for father,
do you remember, dear brother?

From thirty some "li" away around the corner of
the mountain skirt,
after finishing his work at the market,
father always came home without fail however
late it might be.

After a cup of rice wine, with a few dried fish
thrown on his back rack,
he would welcome us with joyful greeting of
"hello, children."
do you remember, dear brother?

Because he never failed to return,
we always waited for him at the entrance of the village,
under the hill beyond the chicken coop.
We waited for him gazing at the innumerable
stars above.

Do you remember our father,
who always comes home?

132

OUR SKIN

To peel the skin,
one must take off the clothing,
for only when we take off the outer covering
can we peel our skin.

When we smear the mud on all over our bodies
and we take off our clothing,
only then, we peel off our skin.

When from the bare skin surface
yellowish betadine is being washed away with water,
then, will the layers of skin be open.
In the tissue of organs among layers,
always we have just one human blood without color.
That is the only blood we can share.

It matters not if bald head,
white, black, red or yellow hair,
whatever the hair color,
for survival of the patient
pulsating arteries need just the blood,
our human blood without color.

Take off our hats and shave off our hair;
take off our clothing and peel off our skin,
then, open our hearts that once were in pain,
open our thoughts that once were closed,
for whenever we share each other through our veins
we all survive.

PEONGCHANG OLYMPICS

At the Gangwon providence,
deep in this mountainous village
as the billions of stars filled the night
the Olympic flame to be lit.
Peongchang, Peongchang!

Wind of the nations of the world
wind of the human spirit
wind of winter through mountains
wind of snow will bring
the noodle of Bongpeong sliding down our throat.
Arirang, Arirang, Arario!

Seeing the pot of spicy fish boiling
getting ready to be served,
why is my friend I met at *Onjeong-ri,

why is the stone face at Ocean Diamond Mountain,
still trapped by the thorn of the DMZ?

May the spirit of the Olympic Peongchang
lift the ugly iron fence off
and stop the mourning of the East Sea.
Are you planning to bring us the meditation of Buddha,
the love of Jesus Christ in harmony?
Arirang, Arirang, Arario!
Let us go over the **Sirirang Hill.

*Onjeong-ri; a Noth Korean village near Diamond Mountain
**Sirirang; the curved hill in an old song

THE LAST STATION
—Hospice

Following the dark-red, thorny pattern of the corridor,
a patient staggers into the hospital room for the
last time.

Ambushed by the pain like a swarm of red ants and
led by fear, the patient lies down side by side
with despair.

One desperate longing, flickers as the image of
peace faintly floated in mirror.
To this image of an infinite benevolence,
the patient pleads the release from the clutch.
For after drying tears,
the patient can stretch the arms and embrace the vast void.

Though trapped in the crevice of a cycle of
birth and death,
there will be time to shed the heavy lead-like
garment of flesh, time for the spirit that has
been hovering nearby to dissipate;
then, there will be time for the pain to
dissolve and for the quiet to descend on the
body that has been writhing in a mire of suffering.

Here at the hospice, the last station of life's
journey, those remaining who shared the pain with the
departing one, now come to share the peace;
with the arms lifted high,
they will embrace heaven in awe and wonderment.

FRIEND

In the picture of his funeral
friend is wearing the silver framed glasses
looking down the auditorium.

In his coffin decorated with flowers
someone is playing guitar
'Your Cheating Heart'.
Singing in his familiar voice
a butterfly is flying away.

On the first day of February
the chicks are looking for the grains,
the snow-mixed rain is falling
spreading the letter of purple,
or orange to the ground.
During the worship of these strangers
I hear the applause of angels.

But the overflow of tears blurs my sight
the hazy fog covers the road he takes,
friend is looking back,
again, again looking back,
surely, I see him leaving with the lonely steps.

POEMS BY SOON PAIK

Soon Paik—Poet, Essayist, Literary Commentator, Columnist, Senior Economist of the US Department of Labor. He was born in Seoul, Republic of Korea, and graduated from Seoul National University (LLD, 1962), Korea University (MA in Economics, 1968), Ohio University (MA in Economics, 1969), West Virginia University (PhD in Economics, 1975).

Washington Spring

Washington spring comes
With an Atlantic Ocean breeze through Chesapeake Bay
Under melting ice of the Potomac River
To the Washington Monument;

Washington spring arrives
By an Appalachian Mountain wind in Shenandoah Valley
On crushing ice of the Blue Ridge streams
To the Lincoln Memorial;

My spring does not come thus far
With sorrow for the division of motherland
For the compassion toward oppressed North Koreans
Into the heart through a whole body;

My spring is yet to be longed for
With an armful of azaleas and the hope of life
Of beautiful news for freedom and unity
Into the spirit through Thee.

WHITE SNOW

White snow sits down silently
On the broad leaves of an evergreen
Boasting a clean purity
Together with the crystal water;

White snow reveals immaculateness glaring
By morning sunlight shining
Like the cotton flower broken out
In the wilderness;

White snow even lays down, putting weight
Upon a branch of the pine tree
Being bent down slightly toward ground
Which supposes to be the weight of a clean purity;

A sparrow flies out of somewhere
And sits down lightly on a branch of the pine tree
Flapping its wings slowly
Touching white snow to fly down onto ground;

A branch of the pine tree leaps up silently toward blue sky
After a white snow falls down without noise to the ground;
Then discover liberty
By dusting off even the weight of a clean purity;

A spirit is open to liberty
As the mind casts away even the intention of becoming a clean purity;
A liberty for love
A liberty for service.

Lake Ann

I keep walking with my wife
On the lane around Lake Ann
Not far from my home;

Communicating with the water of the Lake
Which reflects the Spring maple tree leaves
On the drawing board of the picture;

Listening to 'The Water Music' by Handel
With flapping sound by the duck wings
On the surface of the wrinkles of green water;

I keep drawing in mind myself
Upon a blue sky over Lake Ann
On the fly of the imagination;

Conversing with the same white cloud and blue sky over the Lake
Seen on the way to this land crossing the Pacific Ocean
With a boy's vision and dream being faded away sometime ago;

Listening to 'The Creation' by Hayden
With the melody that the white cloud is a hope
For the truth of the Creation;

I keep appreciating with myself
Watching a family of ducks on one line of togetherness
Toward the horizon of Lake Ann;

Dialoging with all the nature of the Lake
Also with all the nature of the Han River
Left a half century ago never-to-be-forgotten;

Listening 'The Ode to Home Town' by Kim Dong Jin
Reflecting on beautifully grown lives along three oceans
And longing for the unified Korean Peninsula.

ANNAPOLIS

On the top of a pier in Annapolis
Standing alone,
Looking over the sky,
Enjoying the wind blowing from the sea;

A comfortable wind on Eastern seashore
Blowing from across the Atlantic Ocean,
Carrying a smell of Western Civilization,
Touching my brunette, not golden, hair;

On the boardwalk at the Annapolis Beach
Walking fascinatingly and beastly,
With my body, my clothes, and my shoes
Full of the American style;

On the sand dunes at the Annapolis Beach
Scribing my name in the clear-cut Korean characters,
Remembering my father and mother,
Knowing that the waves of tide may erase it without a trace;

On the top of a pier in Annapolis
Standing alone,
Asking to the waves of tide from the Atlantic Ocean
How long my son and his descendents keep their names in Korean.

LET THE SCREAM OF SORROW CRY OUT

In a mountain town encircled by the Appalachians,
At a campus field full of lectures and readings,
A sound of destruction comes from the world
Cracking and screeching a fresh stillness of April green;

American sons and daughters fall down on the clean lawn
Who shall prophesy on new values,
Who shall see visions on the challenge to technology,
Who shall dream dreams on everlasting peace;

Let the scream of sorrow cry out
Memorizing their names inscribed on the blue sky at the campus
With the bloody pieces of flesh
And the crushed fragments of bone;

Moms and Dads
Who come rushing over hundreds of miles with a gun-shot report,
Friends and lovers
Who come running with tears and fear of losing lives of the loved ones,

Let the talk of comfort spread out
Consoling their miserable minds
Who lost the sons and daughters
And friends and lovers;

A day will come
When their swords shall be beaten into plowshares,
When their spears shall be beaten into pruning hooks,
When their hatred shall be transformed into love;

Let the trumpet of peace sound loudly
Putting the eternal rest upon the mortified souls,
Making the sorrow be the joy,
From the heavens.

WAIKIKI BEACH

On the sand dune of Waikiki beach
Through the creative sun rays above the Pacific Ocean,
Sea gulls and pigeons and sparrows walk around nervously
Searching for their breakfast food earnestly,
Pushing their beaks enthusiastically;

On the round desk of the East-West Centre conference room
Under the beautiful chandelier with native decorations,
Men and women and elders and youths talk seriously
Looking for the theories of East-West International affairs,
Discussing loudly for the conclusion to World problems;

From the horizon far above the sea
Over the sand field of the Waikiki seashore,
Sea winds breeze gently and clearly
Delivering the knowledge searched from the sea sand by the sea birds,
Communicating the wisdom found from the sea water by the sea wind.

HAWAII NATIONAL LAVA PARK

Who carves the black sculptures
On the huge plateau of mountains over the Pacific Ocean,
Bringing out the burnt soil from the earth far below,
Spouting up the eruption of rocks from the center of the World;

The sculptures pattern the godly design
On the background of the vast plains and blue sea,
Boasting loudly their wonders through the brisk sea wind,
Revealing clearly their miracles under the splendor of sun;

The faces are distorted devilishly and the bodies twisted crazily
By the flowers of sulfur fires from the bottomless depth,
Showing the dirty figures of human lives,
Revealing the reality of human sinful nature;

A fresh green grass sprout stands alone briskly
Upon the black wilderness burnt out by the volcano fires,
Waving its leaves through the July wind of the Hawaiian Islands,
Appearing wildly the loneliness of life, toward above.

MEETING FATHER

On the way toward the Geum Gang Mountain,
Leaving the Sok Cho Harbor,
Meeting father for the first time in some sixty years;

On the day when a thunderstorm poured loudly from the North,
Taking away father from his room in Won Nam Dong,
Saving behind his compassionate smiles in the hearts of family;

On the dock of the Jang Jin Harbor,
Breezing the spring wind full of azalea fragrance,
Through the Ok Ryu Dong Valley with ten-thousands figures;

On the interview table of the On Jung Ri Village,
Meeting father who might be so old and so feeble,
Expecting his benign face hung up on the wall of the
Won Nam Dong family room;

On his picture of silence,
Revealing his generously smiling face and his spectacled eyes,
With his brown hair and his mustache;

On the Geum Gang Mountain,
Blowing away the vision of meeting father by the mountain brisk wind,
Waiting always for the dreams dreaming the father met a thousand times.

RAIN DROPS

Rain drips spottily on the car front window,
Knocking the sorrow heart
On the way toward the emergency room of the hospital,
Embracing wife groaning of high fever;

Light dangles in the rain drops on the window,
Reflecting some days spent at West Virginia Morgantown
Into the water of the Monongahela Mountain Lake,
Immersing the legs with fishes following;

Rain spots loudly on the car ceiling glass,
Composing the melody of comfort
Inside the depressed minds,
Sounding a voice from heaven;

Rain drips still spottily on the car front window,
Knocking the sorrow heart
On the way home,
Leaving wife with a stable sleep in the hospital bed;

Rain spots still loudly on the car ceiling glass
Pounding strongly the window of the heart
Inside the awakened spirit,
Sounding a chorus of thanksgiving;

Rain drops are love,
Rain drops are comfort,
Rain drops are life,
Rain drops thanksgiving.

LET THE RIVER OF TEARS FLOW

On the way toward the prayer house,
Dashing out through the darkness in the West Virginia Mountains,
Let the river of tears flow;

In the village inside the valley under the star lights,
To you longing for heavenly love in the spirit,
Let the river of tears flow;

On the bed of the sick room under the dim lights,
To you searching for the comfort to the pains of body and soul,
Let the river of tears flow;

On the town in the wilderness of the Du Man River, to you sold out
as a hostage for stealing a piece of bread for her younger brother,
Let the river of tears flow;

In the prayer room waiting for the sunlight breaking the night darkness,
To you praying loudly with all your spirit for His grace and His mercy,
Let the river of tears flow.

CPSIA information can be obtained at www.ICGtesting.com
Printed in the USA
BVOW08s1341101213

338663BV00003B/15/P